Y0-EGC-384

HOW DOES IT FLY? HOW DOES IT FLY? HOW DOES IT FLY?

COMMUNITY · CONNECTIONS

?

Published in the United States of America by Cherry Lake Publishing
Ann Arbor, Michigan
www.cherrylakepublishing.com

Content Adviser: Jacob Zeiger, Production Support Engineer, the Boeing Company

Photo Credits: Cover and page 1, ©Dwight Smith/Shutterstock, Inc.; page 5, ©Patrick Allen/Dreamstime.com; page 7, ©Dan Simonsen/Shutterstock, Inc.; page 9, ©Nicholas Rjabow/Shutterstock, Inc.; page 11, ©iStockphoto/GoosePhotographic; page 13, ©iStockphoto/Linda Braceland; page 15, ©RTimages/Shutterstock, Inc.; page 17, ©corepics/Shutterstock, Inc.; page 19, ©Sergey Kamshylin/Shutterstock, Inc.; page 21, ©iStockphoto/Brian Brown.

On the Cover: The World War II P-40 fighter plane with shark's mouth painted on its nose is a propeller plane.

LIBRARY OF CONGRESS CATALOGING-IN-PUBLICATION DATA
Masters, Nancy Robinson.
  How does it fly? Propeller plane/by Nancy Robinson Masters.
    p. cm.—(Community connections)
  Includes bibliographical references and index.
  ISBN-13: 978-1-61080-070-9 (lib. bdg.)
  ISBN-10: 1-61080-070-2 (lib. bdg.)
  1. Propeller-driven aircraft—Juvenile literature. I. Title. II. Title: Propeller plane.
  TL547.M353 2011
  629.133'343—dc22   2010051451

Cherry Lake Publishing would like to acknowledge the work of The Partnership for 21st Century Skills. Please visit www.21stcenturyskills.org for more information.

Printed in the United States of America
Corporate Graphics Inc.
July 2011
CLFA09

CONTENTS

HOW DOES IT FLY?

TAKE OFF!

The pilot in the airplane **cockpit** calls out "Clear!" He is about to start the engine.

Power from the engine turns the **propeller**. The propeller is a long blade attached to the airplane engine. The spinning propeller scoops air as it turns. This pulls the airplane forward down the runway.

The engine turns the propeller very fast before the airplane starts down the runway.

The pilot pulls back on the controls. The wings lift the airplane into the sky! The power from the engine keeps the propeller spinning. It pulls the airplane forward through the air. The airplane is soon out of sight.

The pilot sits inside the airplane cockpit behind the spinning propeller.

Can you swim?
Think of the propeller
pulling the airplane
through the air. Now
imagine a swimmer
doing the backstroke.
He pulls his arms
through the water.
How are a swimmer's
arms like a
propeller? How are
they different?

7

FOUR FORCES

Four forces act like a tug-of-war on propeller airplanes. **Gravity** pulls the airplane down. **Lift** pushes the airplane up. **Thrust** moves the airplane forward. **Drag** slows the airplane down.

You cannot see these forces. You only see how the propeller airplane reacts to them.

A pilot uses the controls and the forces you can't see to make the airplane roll.

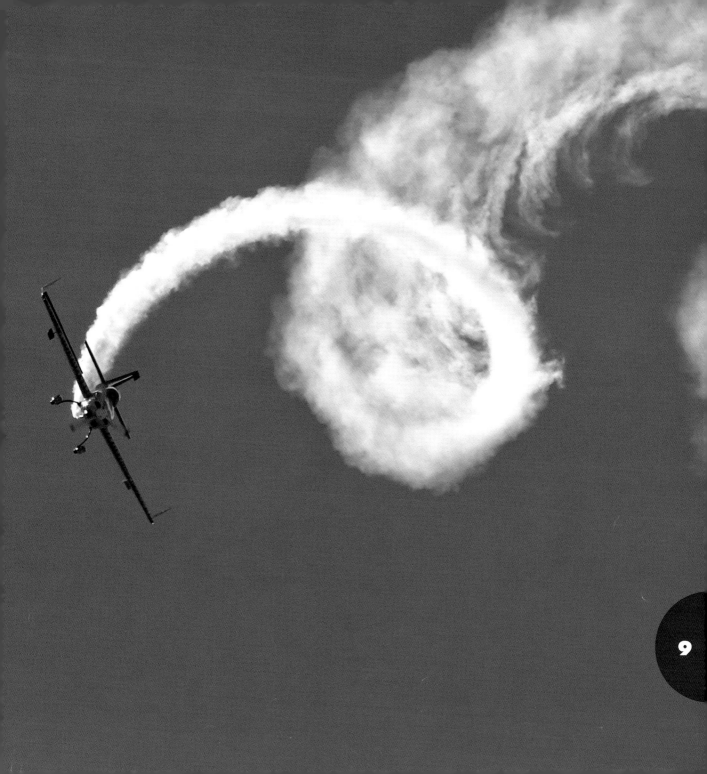

Gravity and lift are opposites. A propeller plane needs lift to fly. The plane takes off when lift is stronger than gravity.

Thrust and drag are also opposites. Thrust has to be stronger than drag for the plane to take off.

Gravity and lift become more equal once the plane is flying. So do thrust and drag.

A plane must gain speed in order to take off.

Propeller planes have **control surfaces** on the wings and the tail. The pilot uses hand or foot controls to move these surfaces.

Air flows across the control surfaces. Moving the control surfaces changes how the air flows across them. This makes the propeller airplane fly up, down, left, or right.

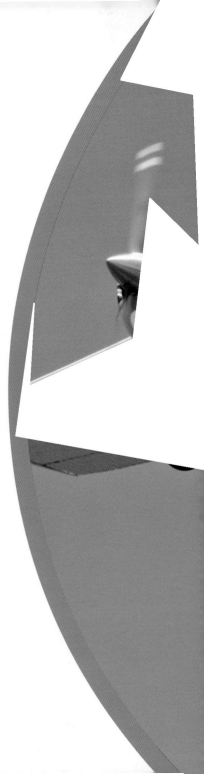

Flaps are control surfaces on the back of the wing. Can you find this airplane's flaps?

Some propeller airplanes have more than one engine. Why do you think some propeller airplanes need more than one engine?

SHAPES AND SIZES

Wings and propellers are **airfoils**. An airfoil is a shape created to direct the flow of air. Wings are curved at the top and flat on the bottom. Air flows faster over the top and slower across the bottom. This creates lift, making the airplane fly.

What do you notice about the shape of this plane's wing?

Inventors Orville and Wilbur Wright created the first airfoil-shaped propeller. They twisted a wing's shape to make a propeller blade. Air flowed evenly across the entire propeller blade.

Propellers are made in different shapes and sizes. They fit the different shapes and sizes of engines. The propeller and engine are the **power plant** of the airplane.

Propeller blades might be long or short. Some are more twisted than others.

The first airplane propellers were made from wood. Most propellers today are made of metal.

Many propellers might be made of **composite** materials in the future. Fiberglass is a composite material made of glass and plastic. Fiberglass and other composites are strong. They weigh less than metal.

This old plane has a new propeller made of metal.

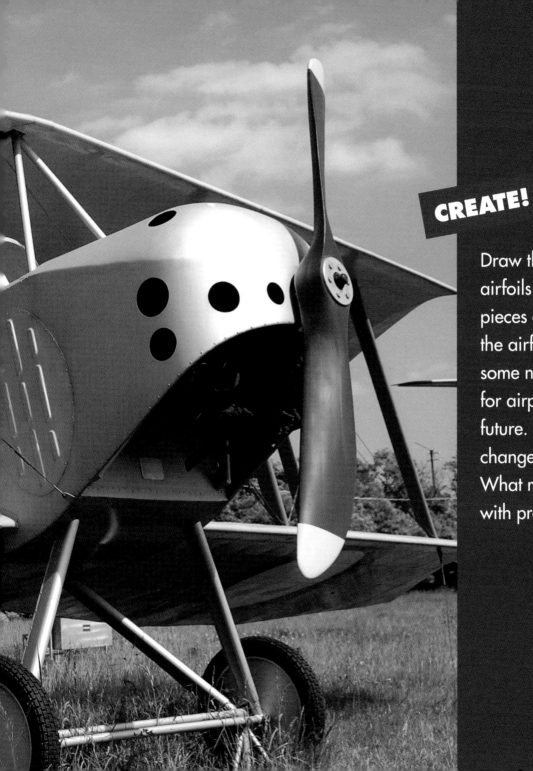

CREATE!

Draw three or four airfoils on different pieces of paper. Use the airfoils to create some new ideas for airplanes of the future. How can you change the wings? What might you do with propellers?

MANY USES

Propeller planes carry passengers and mail. They drop water to put out fires. They take medicine to hospitals. Scientists use propeller planes to learn about the weather. Farmers use them to drop seeds or spray crops to kill insects.

But are they fun to fly? Ask a pilot and he or she will say yes!

A propeller plane can quickly cover large sections of crops.

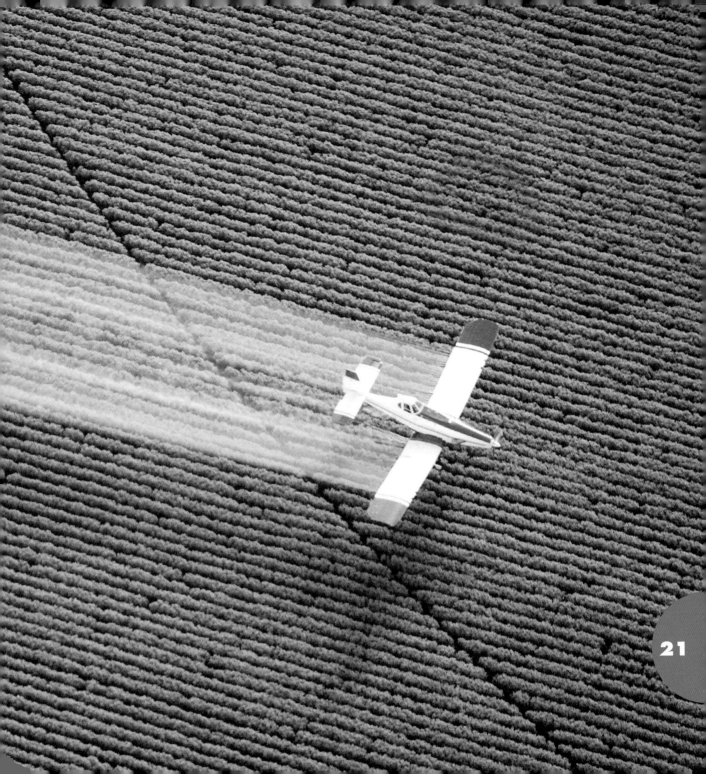

GLOSSARY

airfoils (AYR-foylz) surfaces shaped with a curved top and flat bottom to direct the flow of air

cockpit (KOK-pit) where the pilot sits in the airplane

composite (kuhm-PAH-zit) a material that is very strong and does not weigh much

control surfaces (kuhn-TROHL SUR-fiss-iz) parts of the airplane wing and tail that move up and down or side to side to direct the airplane

drag (DRAG) the force that slows down a moving object

gravity (GRAV-uh-tee) the force that pulls objects toward Earth

lift (LIFT) the upward force of flight

power plant (POw-ur PLANT) the engine and propeller that produce power

propeller (pruh-PEL-ur) a blade or blades shaped like a wing

thrust (THRUHST) the forward force of flight

FIND OUT MORE

BOOKS

Masters, Nancy Robinson. *Airplanes*. Ann Arbor, MI: Cherry Lake Publishing, 2009.

O'Sullivan, Robyn. *The Wright Brothers Fly*. Washington, DC: National Geographic, 2007.

Glover, David, and Penny Glover. *Planes in Action*. New York: PowerKids Press, 2008.

WEB SITES

Smithsonian National Air and Space Museum: Forces of Flight
www.nasm.si.edu/exhibitions/gal109/htf/activities/forcesofflight/web/index.html
Watch a terrific video for kids illustrating the four forces of flight.

Young Eagles
www.youngeagles.org/games/
Check out fun ways to learn more about propeller airplanes.

INDEX

ABOUT THE AUTHOR

Nancy Robinson Masters is an airplane pilot. She loves writing about propeller airplanes. Her husband, Bill, is also a pilot. He teaches people how to fly propeller airplanes. Nancy and Bill live at an airport near Abilene, Texas.